The Chronicles of Christian Grace

Can't Wait to Grow Up

Story by Terence and Eardie Houston

Illustrations by Laura Acosta

Edited by Megan Louw

TDR Brands Publishing

Copyright ©2017 Living Life with the Houston's

All rights reserved. No part of this work may be reproduced or transmitted in any form or by any means, electronic or mechanical, including photocopying and recording or by any information storage or retrieval system, except as may be expressly permitted by the 1976 Copyright Act or in writing from the publisher. Requests for written permission should be addressed in writing to

Living Life with the Houston's
14019 SW Freeway
Suite 301-197
Sugar Land, TX 77478

Please visit www.livinglifewiththehoustons.com to get connected

Printed in the United States of America

ISBN 978-1-947574-25-0

Pamela Massey, LaMonica Love, Paula Whitfield, Priscilla Booker, Chelsea Auguste, LaToshia Norwood, & Joni Clark. Thank you for witnessing the beginning of this journey.

The Chronicles of Christian Grace

Can't Wait to Grow Up

Can't Wait to Grow Up

It was early in the morning and Christian and her big brothers, Joshua and David, were sitting at the table eating their bowls of ooey, gooey, yummy, warm oatmeal and fruit. Joshua and David's spoons were going CLING, CLANG, CLING in their bowls as they ate.

"OK, Everyone," said Daddy, "It's almost time to leave for school. Are you finished with your breakfast?"

The boys had eaten all their oatmeal and all their fruit. "Yes!" they said together. Daddy looked at Christian's bowl, and it still had a lot of ooey, gooey oatmeal in it! Daddy looked at Christian's plate, and there were still four bright red strawberries and two whole slices of apple on it!

"Christian, what's the matter?" Daddy asked. "Is your oatmeal too hot?" It is very important to eat your breakfast and Daddy knew that.

"No," Christian replied quietly, "I just don't want it." She pushed her bowl and plate away.

"Ok, Sweetheart, well, at least eat your fruit," Daddy said as he picked up the bowl of warm oatmeal. "You can eat breakfast again when you get to school."

It was time to leave for school. Joshua and David looked very smart in their matching school uniforms! Christian did not have a school uniform. She wore a pretty green dress with matching socks and a bright yellow backpack shaped like a cute bunny.

"Joshua, you didn't spill anything on your shirt, did you?" asked Mommy as she quickly inspected him. Joshua looked up at Mommy and said, "No, Mommy, my uniform is still clean." Joshua was very proud of his clean uniform.

Christian tugged at Mommy's pants and asked, "Mommy, why don't I have a uniform?"

Mommy was surprised. "Christian, you get to wear your pretty dress!" she said. "You don't need a uniform for school." "What about my backpack?" Christian asked, looking at Joshua and David's matching backpacks.

"What's wrong with your backpack?" asked Daddy. "It's just the right size for you." Daddy winked at Christian.

Christian thought to herself, "But it's for babies." Christian didn't want to be a baby. She wanted to be big just like her brothers.

Christian and the rest of the Houston family all climbed into the car. Everyone put on their safety belts, CLICK, CLICK, CLICK, CLICK. David helped Christian put on her safety belt in her car seat, CLICK, and off they went. They arrived at Joshua and David's school and the boys hopped out.

"Have a great day at school guys; remember to be a light!" called Daddy as he waved at the boys. "Bye, Daddy & Mommy! Bye, Christian!" the boys called out together before they ran on to the school playground. Christian watched them run and wished she was big like they were.

As they drove away, Christian had something to say. "Mommy, I want to go to school with David & Joshua," she announced from the back seat.

Mommy turned around and smiled at Christian. "I know, Christian," she said. "And you will when it's time for you to go to kindergarten. In the meantime, you get to have fun with your friends at your school!"

"But I want to have fun with my brothers! Why can they go, but I can't? It's not fair!" Christian huffed. She felt like a big girl so why couldn't she go to the big school? "It's fair, Christian," answered Daddy. "Your brothers used to go to your school when they were younger. When they turned 5, they went to the bigger school, and when you turn 5, you will too."

Christian's friends were running around the classroom when Christian, Mommy and Daddy arrived at her school. Christian's friends were playing tag and having fun, but she didn't want to play. Christian was upset and held onto Daddy's legs very tightly.

"Hi Christian!" said one of Christian's classmates. "Good Morning, Christian!" smiled Christian's teacher. "Are you ready to have a great day?"

"No!" Christian shouted, "I'm not going to have a great day until I go to big school with my brothers! My insides are sad because I want to have fun with my big brothers. I don't want to go to the baby school anymore!" She buried her face in Daddy's legs and refused to let go!

"Christian!" Mommy said. Mommy was very surprised by Christian's behavior.

Mommy knelt next to Christian and looked her in the eyes. "Christian, thank you for telling us how you feel inside," said Mommy quietly. "I know you sometimes feel sad because you don't do everything that your older brothers do. It's ok to feel that way. But guess what?!"

"What?" Christian mumbled. She didn't think that anything could make her feel better.

"Your brothers don't get to do everything that you do!" Mommy said. "Sometimes, you get to do fun stuff that they don't do."

Christian couldn't believe this! She thought that big kids got to do whatever they wanted!

"Like play soccer with my friends?" she asked. Christian loved soccer. She loved to run and kick the ball around.

"Yes, like play soccer with your friends," answered Mommy. "And other things that you get to do right here at your school! Christian, it's not a baby school, because you're not a baby. It is for younger children and it's a place made for special little girls just like you!"

"Just for me?!" Christian asked as she smiled a big smile. That made her feel very special!

"Just for you," Daddy said as he knelt next to Mommy. "Okayyyy," Christian said as she shared a very big hug with Mommy and Daddy.

After school was over for Christian, Mommy and the boys came to pick her up. When she saw them, she ran over as quickly as she could, her little shoes going PAT, PAT, PAT, PAT on the ground.

"Mommy! David! Joshua!" squealed Christian. She was very happy to see them, and she gave them all a hug.

"Hi, Christian!" smiled Mommy. "How was your day?" Christian was so excited she could hardly breathe! "I had a great day!" she said, speaking very quickly. "We had so much fun! I played with Nia on the playground. And we played the piano during music time. And I learned my colors in Spanish and sign language!"

David looked very impressed and said, "Wow, Christian, that's really cool!"

"Yeah, you're such a big girl, Christian." agreed Joshua. "Babies can't do that."

"That's right." said Christian with her hands on her hips. "I'm not a baby. I'm a big girl, and I'm happy that my school is a special place just for me!"

"But," she said, turning to Mommy, "I'll be even more happy when I can go to school with David and Joshua." Mommy rolled her eyes playfully and laughed, "Oh, Christian!"

The End

"Young people, it's wonderful to be young! Enjoy every minute of it…"

Ecclesiastes 11:9

The Houston's reside in Houston, Texas and are on a mission to educate, inspire, and serve their community.

Please visit www.livinglifewiththehoustons.com to join our community and let us know what you think. Send your feedback, inquiries, collaboration opportunities to contact@livinglifewiththehoustons.com.

Join our email newsletter today for a free surprise from David, Joshua and Christian!

Keep enjoying fun stories with other books from the series "Adventures of David and Joshua" and "The Chronicles of Christian Grace".

To request bulk orders or book signing request, please visit our website.

www.ingramcontent.com/pod-product-compliance
Lightning Source LLC
LaVergne TN
LVHW072128070426
835512LV00002B/41